365 Days Of Inspirational Quotes:
A Year Of Daily Inspiration, Happiness, Success and Motivation.

Barclay Hansen

Content Page

Free Gift

As a thank you for purchasing this book I would like to give you a free gift. It is my PDF action guide titled Beginners Guide To Affirmations: Everything You Need TO Get Started With Affirmations. It is a quick read and is perfect for anyone that wants to start improving their life with affirmations, inside I cover the basics of affirmations, Affirmative Prayer, Cosmic Ordering, Creative Visualization, Mantras and How to build your positive mindset.

https://lifeaffirmations.net/free-gift

Introduction

Inspirational quotes are the perfect way to start the day and set you up for a day of success and accomplishments. Inside the pages of this book you will find a range of quotes to give you a daily dose of Inspiration, Happiness, Success and Motivation.

Use this book to start your day on the right foot, to fill you with happiness before bed or any time during the day when you need a boost of inspiration to help you succeed with whatever the day throws at you.

No matter the circumstance you find yourself in we have quotes to pick you up or keep you motivated to be the best version of yourself.

Quotes

#1
It's Only When You Have The Courage To Step Off The Ledge That You'll Realize You've Had Wings All Along.

#2
Adversity Is But A Gentle Hand To Shape You Into Something Greater.

#3
Negative People Present Us With An Expedited Personal Growth Opportunity.

#4
The Older We Get, The Greater Importance We Place On Time Spent With Loved Ones.

#5
Money Doesn't Change People, But Rather, Only Amplifies That Which A Person Already Is.

#6
Sometimes The Lesson Is In Asking The Question, Not In Finding The Answer

#7
When We Realize We Only Have 86,400 Seconds Each Day And When They're Gone, They're Gone It Makes Us More Conscious Of The Value Of Time.

#8
Many Proudly Say They Don't Fear Death, Yet Live Their Lives As If They Fear Living.

#9
Never Let The Quality Of The Music Determine The Quality Of The Dance.

#10
Rather Than Telling Others How To Live Their Life, Lovingly Show Them By Example.

#11
To Believe Is To Know In Your Heart That It's
Already Done.

#12
Miracles Can Happen From Just Sending
Wishes Of Loving Kindness To Another.

#13
Whether We Tell Ourselves "Life Is Hard" Or
"Life Is Easy", We'll Be Right.

#14
Don't Wait Until You Lose Something To
Realize How Much You Have To Be Grateful
For In This Moment.

#15
Not Making A Choice IS Making A Choice And
It's Not Always The Best One.

#16
Carrying Yesterday's Problems With You Today Is Like Trying To Fly While Carrying A Sack Of Rocks.

#17
When We Give Without Being Asked Miracles Happen.

#18
If Your Dreams Don't Scare You Just A Little Bit, You're Not Playing Big Enough In The World.

#19
We Have A Choice To Make Time For Silence To Hear God's Whisper, Or Wait For Him To Get Our Attention With A Sledgehammer.

#20
When We Focus On Faith Rather Than Fear, Anything Becomes Possible.

#21

Nature Is The Universe's Way Of Making Sure We Remember The Magnificence Of Who We Really Are.

#22

Never Allow The Size Of Your Dreams To Be Limited By What Someone Else Thinks Is Possible.

#23

If You're Going To Take The Time To Do It, Do It Right The First Time.

#24

You Are A Spiritual Being Enjoying A Human Experience, Part Of Something So Much Greater That Will Live Forever.

#25

Be Present And Remember To Breathe.

#26
Adversity Is But An Opportunity, Not An Excuse.

#27
You'll Always Find What You're Looking For, Either The Good Or The Bad, In Any Situation... But Finding The Good Is More Fun.

#28
The Nutritional Choices We Make Today Will Directly Affect The Health Of Our Bodies Tomorrow. Choose Wisely

#29
Enjoy The Journey, Knowing That What Appears To Be The Shortest Path Isn't Always The Best Route.

#30
Rather Than Seeking Gratification, Which Is Fleeting, Create Lasting Fulfillment Instead.

#31

Meditate And Pray On Understanding, Not Outcome, Knowing There Is Blessing In Everything.

#32

Inspire Others To Be Their Best By First Being YOUR Best.

#33

The Greatest Gift You Can Ever Give To Others Is The Gift Of Just Being You.

#34

Be Grateful, For From Gratitude Alone The Magic Of The Universe Will Be Revealed To You.

#35

Think Without Boundaries. Dream Without Limitations.

#36

Life Is Like A Trapeze: You Have To Let Go Of
One Place To Get To Another. Swing,
Release, Catch... Swing, Release, Catch

#37

What If All Your Problems Could Be Solved By
One Tiny Idea? The Answer Is Within Pay
Attention
And Listen.

#38

Rather Than Rowing Your Own Boat, Take
Action By Setting Your Sails And Stepping Into
The Wind. Sail On!

#39

If We Could Stand In Another's Shoes, We
Wouldn't Be So Quick To Judge One Another
Ever Again.

#40

In Retrospect, Some Of The Greatest
Blessings In My Life Have Come From
Adversity

#41
Seek Knowledge While Knowing That All The
Answers To All The Questions Are Already
Inside Of You.

#42
When You Can Be Happy Right Now, In Spite
Of Problems, You'll Find They Disappear
Much More Quickly

#43
If You Can See The Life Of Your Dreams It
Tends To Show Up Even Faster. Dream It.
See It. Live It!

#44
You Are The Painter Of The Masterpiece
Called Life, And Your Attitude Is The Brush.

#45
Collaboration Is The New Way. Competition
Only Exists In Our Minds. There's Plenty For
All Of Us

#46
Circumstances Can't Affect Whether Or Not You Are Happy, When Your Happiness Is Not Dependent Upon A Reason.

#47
Dream Incessantly, Believe Completely, Act Daily, Celebrate Continually.

#48
What's Happening Outside Of You Is Irrelevant Compared To What's Happening Inside.

#49
When Our Burning Desire For Success Is Greater Than Our Deepest Fear Of Failure, We Have The Power To Create Anything In Our Life!

#50
It Helps To Know That As We Go Through Painful Times, We Get To Choose How To Respond To Them.

#51
Sometimes We Need To Be Reminded That We Are Spiritual Beings Having A Human Experience.

#52
No Matter What It Might Feel Like, Know That You Are Never Alone.

#53
You Touch Everyone You Interact With In Either A Positive Or Negative Way. Make It Positive.

#54
When You Can Look At A Coming Storm In The Face Without Fear, You Have Mastered Your Life.

#55
Where Focus Goes, Energy Flows

#56
On This Beautiful Day, Take Time To Be
Grateful, For From That Alone, The Magic Of
The Universe Will Be Revealed To You.

#57
It's Not About Who Gets There First, But
Who's Had The Most Fun On The Journey.

#58
Luck Isn't Something That Happens To You,
It's Something You Create

#59
Bless Your Enemies. Forgive Others And
Yourself. You Can't Swim With An Anchor Tied
To Your Feet.

#60
In The Midst Of Constant Change, The One
Thing That Remains The Same Is The
Essence Of Who We Are And The Greater
Sense Of Knowing Found Deep Within
Ourselves.

#61
The Fact That We Share The Same Fears
Should Unite Us, Not Divide Us.

#62
Think Good Thoughts. Do Good Things. Be
Good To The World And To Yourself. Easy

#63
The World Needs You To Live Out Your
Dream, As No One Can Sing Your Song Or
Dance Your Dance Quite Like You Can

#64
Change Happens First In Our Mind, Then In
Our World. Believe It And Then You'll See It.

#65
We Stumble, We Fall, We Get Back Up Again.
Guess Which Part Is The Most Important?

#66
You're Taking A Deep Breath Doesn't Diminish My Air Supply Any More Than Your Success Prevents Mine. We Are Abundance.

#67
When Everything We Do Comes From A Place Of Love Rather Than Fear, We Will Have Achieved Peace On Earth.

#68
Focus On What You Want, Not What You Don't Want. Simple, Easy.

#69
Rather Than Asking, "What's The Worst That Could Happen?", Instead, Ask Yourself, "What's The BEST That Could Happen?"

#70
The Fastest Way To Get From Fear To Abundance Is By A Shortcut Called Gratitude.

#71
Follow Your Passion, Listen To Your Dreams, Believe In Yourself And All Good Things Will Come Your Way.

#72
As We Grow, The Obstacles In Our Path Shrink In Proportion, So That What Once Appeared As A Boulder Becomes A Mere Stepping Stone.

#73
Believing That You Lack Abundance Is Like A Fish Believing That It Lacks Water. You Are Abundance.

#74
Your Life Will Improve Exponentially When You Improve The Life Of Another.

#75
Dream Big And Make Life Fun! Do Something Outrageous Each Day.

#76
If You Must Follow Something Rather Than Lead, Let It Be Your Own Bliss.

#77
The Fear Of The Storm Is Always Worse Than The Storm Itself.

#78
Our Strength And Resilience Are Always In Direct Proportion To Our Level Of Adversity

#79
Sometimes We Forget Who We Are. Remember You Are An Infinite Being With Unlimited Possibility

#80
Live Your Life With No Regrets. Bless The Past And Let It Go.

#81

It's Easy To Show Kindness And Love Others
When You First Love Yourself.

#82

Just The Fear Of Failure, Not Failure Itself,
Has The Ability To Stop Greatness In Its
Tracks.

#83

To Achieve Success, Attitude Is More
Important Than Assets, Aptitude, Age Or
Anything Else.

#84

Follow Your Heart, Not Your Fears. Fear Is
Nothing More Than False Evidence Appearing
Real.

#85

The Only Thing That Makes A Good Day
Different From A Bad Day, Is Simply Our
Perception.

#86
Live Simply, Love Deeply And Know Your Own Inner Wisdom.

#87
When We Think With No Limits, We Allow God To Show Us A Bigger, Better Dream Of Possibility.

#88
If You Are Worthy Of The Breath Of Life, You Are Worthy Of All Else. Let It In.

#89
Send A Blessing Today To The Person In Your Life Who You'd Least Want To Bless, And See What Happens. Love Is Always The Answer.

#90
The Gift Of Oneself Is The Greatest Thing We Can Give. Be Present.

#91
When You Feel Sad Or Stuck, Remember
Your Life Can Change In The Flash Of A
Moment, And Perhaps That Moment Is Now.

#92
Believe That You Can Do It, For When You
Believe, Doors Will Open Unto You.

#93
The Worst Things That Ever Happen To Us
Are The Stories We Tell Ourselves. Misery
Comes Only From Believing Our Thinking.

#94
When You're Able To Look At The World As
Cooperative Rather Than Competitive,
Everything Changes And There Is Enough For
Everyone.

#95
Every Day, If We Find Someone Who's Having
A Bad Day And Send Them Some Love, We
Just Might Change The World.

#96
When We Learn To Label Challenging Situations Or Problems As Fascinating Rather Than Frustrating, Something Shifts Within That Allows The Solution To Reveal Itself.

#97
Miracles First Show Up As Baby Steps Of Possibility.

#98
For All Things, For All Reasons, Express Your Gratitude.

#99
Do Something Special To Inspire Someone Else Today, And Chances Are, It Will Touch Your Life Too.

#100
A Positive Attitude Can Overcome A Negative Situation.

#101

For Every Thought You Have Today, Unseen Forces Will Line Up To Make It Happen For You, So, Think Good Thoughts.

#102

Nothing Is Greater Than LOVE. Spread Some Today.

#103

May Peace And Understanding Be Yours In This Moment.

#104

Kindness And Love Will Conquer Fear And Illusion Any Day.

#105

Dream Incessantly, Believe Completely, Act Daily, Risk Intuitively, Celebrate Continually.

#106
Nothing Eliminates Pain And Difficulty In Our Life Faster Than A Greater Purpose.

#107
Happiness Is Something That Happens From A Choice Within, Rather Than From Circumstance Outside Of Ourselves.

#108
For The Next Hour, Disconnect. Rather Than Being Available To The World, Realize That You ARE The World.

#109
The Most Important Person To Love, Is YOU. Once You Do That, It's Easier To Love Everyone Else.

#110
We Have A Finite Amount Of Time, So The More We Worry, The Less Time We Have To Dream. For Me, I Think I'd Rather Dream

#111
It Is Your Attitude That Will Determine Your Altitude In Life. Confidence And Optimism Will Take You To The Top Of The Mountain.

#112
Never, Ever Give Up On Your Dreams. Never, Ever!

#113
You Don't Have The Ability To Change The Wind, But You Get To Choose How To Trim Your Sails.

#114
Wake With Gratitude, Work With Joy, Live With Integrity, Play With Gusto And Insomnia Will Never Be A Problem.

#115
Limitations Are Nothing More Than Artificial Boundaries That We Create To Feel Safe. Remember, You Can Do Anything!

#116
If I Have Any Regrets At The End Of My Life, I Want Them To Be For The Things I Did Do, Not Those That I Didn't.

#117
Praise Is One Of The Best Inexpensive Gifts We Can Shower On Others. Catch Someone Doing Something Right.

#118
Live To Give And Give To Life. Giving Is The Reason For Living.

#119
What We Choose To Do In Each Moment Defines Where We're Going In Our Life.

#120
Belief, Not Worry, Is The Only Way Out Of A Bad Situation.

#121
The Problem Is Not That There Are Problems.
The Problem Is Expecting Otherwise And
Thinking That Having Problems Is A Problem.

#122
Thinking That We Have To Create Abundance
Is Like Thinking We Have To Create Sunshine.
We ARE Abundance.

#123
A Single Candle Can Light The Way For The
Masses. Today, Shine Brightly.

#124
There Is Greater Value In Implementation
Than In Simply Having An Idea. Make It
Happen.

#125
Anything Is Possible. The Most Audacious
Dreams Can Be Realized, By Intention,
Preparation, Action And Unwavering Belief.

#126
Focus On What You DO Have Instead Of
What You Don't.

#127
The More You Worry, The Less You Dream.
Choose To Dream.

#128
Go With The Flow And Be Willing To Allow
Change Into Your Life, For Change Is The
Only Thing That's Constant.

#129
You Only Lose When You Give Up.

#130
No Matter The Question, Love Is Always The
Answer. Start There First And Watch Magic
Unfold.

#131
The Only Way To Bring Something Into Your Life Is To First Believe That It's Possible, For Without Vision And Belief, Nothing Happens.

#132
For All That You Do, And All That You Are, No One Deserves Loving Kindness Today More Than You Do.

#133
Life Is Richer When We Celebrate Our Successes Rather Than Focusing On Our Failures.

#134
Nothing Can Dissipate Adversity Faster Than Changing Your Focus.

#135
Happiness Is A Choice That You Get To Make.

#136
What's Possible For You In Your Life? Ask.
Trust. Infinite Possibilities Are Born Of Faith.

#137
The First Step To Loving Someone Is
Understanding Who They Are. Listen With
Your Heart.

#138
Every Day, Dream And Be Inspired. Read A
Good Story, Sing A Song, Play In Nature And
Share Love.

#139
Do Something Today That Makes You Grow.
Stretch Your Boundaries And Reach Outside
Of The Box.

#140
May You Be Safe, May You Be Happy, May
You Be Healthy, May You Live With Ease And
Know That You Are Loved.

#141
Rather Than Fighting The Wind, It's Much
Easier To Trim The Sails.

#142
Everything Happens For A Reason, Even If
You Don't Understand It In The Moment.

#143
Even If You Don't Know How To Complete A
Project, Just Take The First Step. There Is
Power In Action.

#144
Serendipity Happens To Us All Every Day. The
Key To The Frequency And Importance Is
Simple: Pay
Attention.

#145
Love's The Only Road To Travel.

#146
Know That The Real Gift You Give Isn't The Presents, It's Your Presence.

#147
The False Beliefs We Have In Our Heads Are Our Only Cause Of Unhappiness. Change Our Thought, Change Our World.

#148
Your Worst Day May Be Someone Else's Best Day. It's All Perspective. How We See Ourselves Changes How We See The World.

#149
If You're Going Through A Rough Time, The Universe Just Might Be Preparing You For Something Greater.

#150
Once You Understand That Abundance Is There For Everyone, Life Gets Much Easier.

#151
Laugh More + Love More = Live A Longer,
Healthier And Happier Life.

#152
Appreciate Where You've Been, Anticipate
Where You're Going, But Most Importantly,
Cherish Where You Are In This Moment.

#153
You Cannot Discover New Lands Unless You
Take Your Ship Out Of The Harbor. Sail On
Brave One!

#154
What You Get From Life Will Be In Direct
Proportion To What You Give TO Life.

#155
We Do Have A Choice In Everything, Every
Day, Even When It Appears That We Don't.

#156
Even Enlightened People Have Problems. The Only Difference Is In Their Reaction To Them

#157
Tomorrow, When You Are A Beautiful Butterfly, It Will Be Hard To Remember Your Days As A Caterpillar.

#158
No One Deserves Loving Kindness Today More Than You Do.

#159
When Your Burning Desire For Success Is Greater Than Your Deepest Fear Of Failure, You Can Create Anything In Your Life!

#160
Happiness Is Found In Your Heart, Not In Your Circumstances.

#161
Live Purposefully. Give Abundantly. Love Unconditionally. Hug Joyfully. Celebrate Gratefully.

#162
Feeling Stuck? The Best Way To Get Unstuck Is To Go Do Something For Someone Else!

#163
Knowing That What We Focus On Grows, Count Your Blessings Instead Of Your Problems.

#164
Just Because No One's Ever Done It Before Doesn't Mean It's Impossible. Go For It!

#165
Love Is The Answer To Any Of Your Questions Today. Just Start There First And Watch Magic Unfold.

#166
Dream Big And Make Life Fun! Do Something Outrageous Each Day. Follow Your Passion. Believe In Yourself.

#167
There Are Few Things In Life That Can't Be Solved By A Bubble Bath.

#168
Play BIG, Make It Fun Or Don't Play At All. Might As Well Make It Worth The Effort, No?

#169
Challenge Is Nothing More Than A Seed Of Opportunity.

#170
Don't Put Off Until Tomorrow That Which You Can Enjoy Today!

#171

All Things Are Possible, If You Never Give Up!

#172

Live In The Present. It's The Only Thing That Truly Exists. Never Look Back Unless You Are Planning To Go That Way.

#173

Love Everyone. Life Is Just Too Short For Anything Else.

#174

Inspiration Is The Rocket Fuel That Makes Ordinary Days Extraordinary.

#175

Take Responsibility For Your Actions And Inactions, Realizing That At All Times, You Get To Choose How To Act Or React.

#176

When You Accept That You're Exactly Where You're Supposed To Be In This Moment And That You Have All That You Need, Miracles Happen.

#177

Adversity Provides The Opportunity For The Best Part Of Us To Shine.

#178

Just As The Birds Receive What They Need Each Day, Live Your Life Knowing That Abundance Is Already Yours.

#179

Today, Please Share Appreciation, Spread The Love And Happiness And Watch What Happens.

#180

Take Love With You In All Things That You Do And Leave Only Ripples Of Kindness Behind You.

#181
When The Purpose Is Big Enough, We Find
The Courage To Move Mountains.

#182
More Forward With Confidence, Knowing In
The Core Of Your Being That You Have The
Power To Achieve Your Dreams.

#183
Sometimes The Only Change We Need Is A
Change In How We See The World.

#184
You Can Only Do One Thing At Any Time;
Dream, Plan Or Worry. Kinda Makes Worry A
Silly Third Choice, No?

#185
You Were Born An Infinite Being With
Unlimited Potential, And You Still Are That
Magnificence.

#186
Love Is All There Is.

#187
Be Not Afraid To Surrender Your Beliefs On How Things "Should" Be, To The Greater Will Of The Universe.

#188
The Quality Of Your Life Will Be In Direct Proportion To The Level Of Your Gratitude.

#189
Blessings Happen More Frequently When We Take The Time To Notice Them.

#190
ALL People Have Adversity. What Separates The Good From The Great Is How We Choose To React To It.

#191
Give To Others With No Expectation Of
Receiving Anything In Return.

#192
When The Dream Is BIG Enough, We Find
The Motivation To Get Through The Tough
Times.

#193
If You've Hit A Wall Or The Door Has Closed,
Keep Looking Until You Find The Window, For
There's Always A Solution.

#194
Let Your Thoughts And Actions Come Only
From A Place Of Love.

#195
Happiness And Love Are Choices That We
Get To Make In Each And Every Moment.

#196
Adversity Is The Universe's Way Of Directing
Us Down A Different Path.

#197
On Your Deathbed, Regrets Are Usually Of
Things You Didn't Do, Not Things You Did! So,
Go Do It!

#198
The Number One Way To Improve Your Life Is
Through The Conscious Practice Of Gratitude.

#199
Life Works Best When We Focus On Where
We're Going Rather Than Where We've Been.

#200
You Are Not The Troubles That Happen To
You. You Are Magnificence Unfolding. Allow It
To Happen.

#201
Each Day, Do Your Best And Let Go Of The Rest.

#202
Love Eradicates Fear Like Light Dispels Darkness, So Shine Your Love On The World!

#203
We Make The Greatest Difference In The World When We Find A Cause That's Bigger Than Our Fears And Step Forward With Faith.

#204
Make A Choice. Change Your Thoughts = Change Your World

#205
We May Not Choose Our Circumstances But We Do Choose Our Attitude And Our Response.

#206
Adversity Happens To Everyone And It Is Not
An Excuse For Abandoning Our Dreams.

#207
Know That There Is Enough For All Of Us,
Enough Money, Enough Opportunity, Enough
Love For All Of Us To Be Happy.

#208
Someone In The World Is Better Off Today
Because Of Something You've Done.

#209
Even If Life Is A Bumpy Road Or Your Dreams
Are Taking A Circuitous Route, Take Time To
Live In The Moment And Enjoy The Scenery
Along The Way.

#210
One Of The Amazing Things About This
Chess Game Called "Life", Is That We Get To
Choose If We Want To Be The Chess Master
Or The Pawn.

#211

Nothing In Life Is To Be Feared, It Is Only To Be Understood.

#212

Choose Consciously And Wisely. You Are Only One Choice Away From Changing Your World.

#213

Success Looks At Adversity As A Step To Something Greater, Not A Wall To Stop Progress.

#214

Just As In Nature Where The Antidote And The Poison Grow Side By Side, You'll Never Be Given A Dream Without The Ability To Make It Happen.

#215

The Best Thing About A Hug Is That When You Give One Away You Still Have An Endless Supply.

#216
You Are An Unlimited Being Filled With Infinite Possibility, With The Power To Be, Do Or Create Anything That You Desire In Your Life.

#217
Make Your Life A Garden Where You Plant Seeds Of Possibility And Water Them With Gratitude.

#218
You Are Divine Energy In Human Form, You Are Only As Limited As Your Thoughts.

#219
Pain May Be Inevitable But Remember, Suffering Is Optional.

#220
Change Your Attitude To "I'll See It When I Believe It", Not The Other Way Around.

#221
Instead Of Cursing The Darkness, Be The One To Light A Candle.

#222
Realize That What's Happening Around You Doesn't Define Who You Are.

#223
Kindness Is God's Reminder That We See Through Our Eyes But Connect Through Our Hearts.

#224
Life Is Magical When We Are Bold And Have The Courage To Move Forward Into The Unknown, Rather Than Backwards Into Security.

#225
Laughter Is Not Only Contagious, But Is Experienced In A Deeper Way When It Is Shared.

#226
Even The Largest Of !Res Starts From A Tiny Spark. That Same Potential Is Within You, So Set Your Dreams On Fire!

#227
You Will Go Through Pain In Your Life, But How You Choose To Respond To It Is Your Choice.

#228
When You Surround Yourself With People Who Support Your Dreams, You Will Achieve Success More Quickly.

#229
Sometimes We May Forget Who We Are. But What Matters Most Is How Quickly We Remember Our Magnificence.

#230
With Laughter Or Love, The More You Give The More You'll Receive.

#231
Live Well, Laugh Often, Love Deeply.

#232
Worry Is The #1 Thief Of Our Time And Has
The Power To Rob You Of Beauty Of Today.

#233
Change Is Inevitable And Those Who Adapt
Quickly Are Most Likely To Succeed.

#234
We Can't Choose The Number Of Our Age,
But We CAN Choose The Age Of Our Attitude.

#235
Adversity Forces Us To Focus On Things We
Need To Learn.

#236
Forget Early, There Are Enough Worms For All Of Us.

#237
Love Is Letting Others Know How Much You Appreciate Them.

#238
Life Works Better When We Go With The Flow Rather Than Fight The Current.

#239
Gratitude, Kindness And Caring Are More Powerful Than Any Problem You Think You Have.

#240
How We See Ourselves Determines How We See The World.

#241
You Can't Worry Yourself Out Of A Bad Situation, But You Can Believe Yourself Out Of It!

#242
Nobody's Perfect. We All Fall Down. What Matters Most Is How Quickly We Get Back Up, Learn From Our Mistakes And Move On!

#243
Realize That You Have The Power To Do, Be Or Create Anything In Your Life. Anything.

#244
The Two Most Powerful Words In Any Language, "Thank You!"

#245
If You Don't Ask For What You Want, The Answer Is Already NO. Why Not Ask, And Maybe The Answer Will Be YES!?

#246
Sometimes The Fastest Way To Reach Your Dream Is To Help Someone Else Reach His Or Her Dream.

#247
With Belief And Action All Things Are Possible.

#248
Imperfect Action Is Better Than Perfect Inaction.

#249
What Would You Do If You Knew That Your Wildest Dreams Could Come True And That You Couldn't Fail?

#250
When We Learn To Find The Blessing In Any Situation, We've Mastered This Journey Called "Life".

#251
Illusions Can Appear Real But We Get To Choose Whether Or Not To Buy Into Them.

#252
Being Kind To You Is Really Being Kind To Me, For We Are But Individual Parts Of The Same Whole.

#253
Beating Yourself Up Doesn't Benefit Anyone. Focus On What You Choose To Create Instead.

#254
Your Thoughts Become Things. You Decide. You Rule. That's Pretty Cool.

#255
May You Be Blessed With Thoughts And Opportunities And Take Action That Will Create Abundance In Your Life.

#256
What Other People Think About You Isn't
About You. It's About Them.

#257
When Universal Timing And Our Timing Are
Different, That Doesn't Mean That Things
Aren't Working. Trust The Process.

#258
What's Happening On The Outside Doesn't
Have The Power The Affect What's Happening
On The Inside, Unless We Allow It To.

#259
We're Only Here To Learn To Love.

#260
Choose To Love With All Your Heart, Even If It
Sometimes Breaks.

#261

We Imagine The Worst. If You're Going To Use Your Imagination, Imagine GOOD Things Happening!

#262

A Decision Is Nothing More Than A Choice To Eliminate Other Options And Follow Your Path With Determination.

#263

Push Yourself To Do One Thing Outside Your Comfort Zone Today.

#264

Adversity Could Be The Greatest Gift In Our Life, In Retrospect.

#265

Abundance Isn't Something That You Have, It's Who You Already Are.

#266
Ask, Give Thanks, Repeat. Ask, Give Thanks, Repeat.

#267
Treat All Others As If The Entire World Were Watching Your Actions.

#268
Each Day Take The Time To Reconnect And Remember, You Are An Infinite Being With Unlimited Potential.

#269
Our Dreams Have No Limitations Except Those That We Place On Them.

#270
The Power To Change The World Starts With Us First Changing Our Belief And Ourselves.

#271

When You Focus On Faith Rather Than Fear,
You Tap Into A Strength To Carry You Over
Even The Tallest Of Mountains.

#272

For The Next Moment, Allow Yourself To Be A
Human Being Rather Than A Human Doing.

#273

Gratitude Must Be Part Magic, For When I Fill
My Heart With Gratitude, Anything Is Possible.

#274

If We Allow Our Definition Of What's Possible
To Be Based On How Big Someone Else Can
Dream, Our Dream Will Die.

#275

It's Impossible To Be Of Service To Others
And Feel Sorry For Yourself. Choose One.

#276
When We Change Our Beliefs On The Inside,
We Will Transform Our Results On Our
Outside World.

#277
If You Wait For Everything To Be Perfect
Before Taking Action On Your Dream, You'll
Never Take The First Step.

#278
"Can't" Isn't A Word. You Have The Power To
Do, Be Or Create Anything.

#279
At The End Of Life We're Going To Ask, Did I
Live? Did I Love? Ask It Now. The Clock Is
Ticking, You'd Better Start Living.

#280
If We Knew How Loved, How Divine, How
Unlimited We Really Are, We'd See One
Another Through Tears Of Joy.

#281
When We Look For The Good And Expect It
To Show Up, We'll Always Find It.

#282
When We Celebrate In Advance, Things Have
A Way Of Lining Up For Us More Quickly.

#283
No Matter What The Past May Look Like,
Without Our Permission, Our Yesterday Does
Not Have The Power To Determine Our
Tomorrow.

#284
Your Actions, Thoughts And Words Today Are
But Seeds For Tomorrow's Garden.

#285
The Shortest Path To Success, Focus On The
'What' And The 'Why', Not The 'How'. Works
Every Time.

#286

To Improve What Shows Up In The Exterior Of Your World, First, Be Still And Improve The Interior.

#287

Problems Do Not Define Who You Are Unless You Allow Them To. Remember Your Magnificence.

#288

We Can Get So Much Further In Life Through Collaboration Rather Than Competition. One Plus One Equals Eleven, Not Two.

#289

Beyond Words, Beyond Actions, Beyond Feelings, Know In Your Core That You Are Loved.

#290

Know That Deep Inside, You Are Resilient, Brave And So Much Stronger And More Powerful Than Your Fears.

#291
Size Matters, So Keep Your Dreams Big And Your Worries Small.

#292
If You Can't Change The Circumstances, Change Your Attitude. Funny Thing Is, When You Do, You'll Find That The Circumstances Then Change.

#293
Don't Let Your Fear Of The Hazards Keep Your Ship In The Harbor. Cast Off Your Lines And Sail Away!

#294
Abundance Flows More Freely To You When It Continues To Flow Outward From You, As You Pass It On.

#295
Fear Less, Hope More; Eat Less, Chew More; Whine Less, Breath More; Talk Less, Say More; Hate Less, Love More; And All Good Things Shall Be Yours.

#296
Chances Are, When You Fall Asleep With A Prayer Of Gratitude On Your Lips, You'll Wake With A Song Of Joy In Your Heart.

#297
We Often Learn Too Late That We Spent Too Much Time Worrying About The Things That Mattered Least.

#298
The More Clear You Are In The Vision Of What You Want In Life, The Brighter The Spotlight Will Be To Lead You On The Right Path.

#299
Find People Who Believe In You Until You Can Believe In Yourself.

#300
Allow Adversity To Be Your Teacher.

#301
Above All Else, Be True To You.

#302
Giving Is The Reason For Living.

#303
Change Your Beliefs And You'll Change Your Thoughts. Change Your Thoughts And You'll Change Your Habits. Change Your Habits And Your Life Opens To Unlimited Possibility.

#304
In This Very Moment You Hold The Power To Change Someone Else's Life For The Better. Go Do It.

#305
Your Expectations For Any Given Situation Will Greatly Influence The End Result

#306
Action Is The Step Many Forget When They Wonder What Happened To Their Dream.

#307
With The Right Attitude Anything Is Possible.

#308
The Music Of Success Is Sweetest When You Play In A Band Of Winners. Surround Yourself With Excellence!

#309
Go Make Your Life The One You Have Always Wanted, Knowing You Have The Power To Make It Happen.

#310
When You Start Your Day With Gratitude Everything Falls Into Place With Grace And Ease.

#311
If You Have To Doubt Something, Let It Be Your Own Perceived Limitations. Expand, Stretch And Believe!

#312
Ah...For The Next Moment, Allow Yourself To Be A Human Being Rather Than A Human Doing. Do Nothing, Just BE. Ah...

#313
Integrity Is Holding Fast To Our Convictions Regardless Of The Consequences And Never Compromising Our Ideals Or Values, Even If It Affects The Bottom Line.

#314
The Fastest Way To Get To The Life You Want Is To Just Play Make Believe That You Already Have It Today.

#315
Take Time Each Day To Connect To The Divine. Trust That There Is A Plan Even If You Only See A Fraction Of It.

#316
Never Underestimate The Power Of An
Unlimited Being…YOU.

#317
Challenging People Are In Your Life For A
Reason, Love Them.

#318
Play And Don't Take Yourself Or The World
So Seriously. Create Reasons To Laugh!

#319
Adversity Can Be Turned To Opportunity
Simply By Adjusting Our Perception And Our
Attitude.

#320
When We Focus On What We Can Do Instead
Of What We Can't, A World Of Possibility
Opens Unto Us.

#321
Change Requires You To Shift Your Identity Of Who You Are.

#322
Start With Your Beliefs, Which Will Lead Your Thoughts, Which Will Create Your Actions, Which Will Produce Your Results.

#323
Remember, You Are An Infinite Being And Deserve A Day Filled With Unlimited Potential.

#324
As You Close Your Eyes Tonight, May You Know How Blessed You Are And Celebrate With Gratitude.

#325
The Greatest Limitations In Life Are The Ones We Place On Ourselves.

#326
We Make Room For Love When We First
Invite Understanding Into Our Hearts..

#327
To Achieve Your Dream, See The World As
You Want It To Be, Not As It May Appear To
Be.

#328
Either Way You're Going Off The Ledge. So
Why Not Jump Now So God Doesn't Have To
Push You? Your Wings Are Beautiful!

#329
You Can Summit The Biggest Mountain By
Simply Taking The First Step.

#330
True Wealth Is Celebrating The Present
Moment.

331
Sometimes The Greatest Gift You Can Give
Another Is To Ask For Help. There Is Pleasure
In Giving.

#332
Success Often Comes To Those Who Are Too
Naïve To Know That What They're Trying To
Do Is Impossible.

#333
The Fastest Way To Get Unstuck Is To Go Do
Something For Someone Else.

#334
Nothing Has The Power To Radically Change
A Life More Than An Attitude Adjustment.

#335
Collaboration And Cooperation Will Beat
Competition Every Time. Think Abundantly.
Speak Authentically. Serve Willingly. You
Have Enough. You Are Enough.

#336
Change Your Thoughts And You'll Change
Your World.

#337
Focus On The WHY Of Life And Not The
HOW, Remembering That Where Focus Goes,
Energy Flows.

#338
Life Is More Meaningful When Our Goal Is
Fulfillment Rather Than Gratification.

#339
Everything Starts From Gratitude. Everything.
From There, All Else Lines Up For You.

#340
For Today, Think Positive Thoughts, Believe In
Yourself And Others, Share Hugs And Spread
Love. That's It, Nothing Else.

#341
Every Good Thing You Do Creates Ripples
That You May Not See. Do Them Anyway.

#342
Remember, Perspective Can Cause Two
People To Look At The Same Thing And See
Two Totally Different Things.

#343
Take The Time Today To Be Good To You, In
Thoughts, Deeds And Actions, But Especially
In Your Thoughts.

#344
Most Times, Regrets Are Things We Didn't Do,
Not Those We Did.

#345
In Times Of Turmoil, It Matters Not That We
Forgot We Are Infinite, Unlimited Beings. What
Matters Most, Is How Quickly We Remember.

#346
There Is Nothing More Important In The World
Than Loving Yourself.

#347
Praise Is One Of The Best, Yet Inexpensive
Gives We Can Give To Others.

#348
Today, Be The Person Of Your Dreams. See
And Act From Their Eyes.

#349
Limitations Seem Real When We Lack Faith
And Belief. With Faith And Belief, Anything Is
Possible.

#350
When Was The Last Time Worry Ever Solved
A Problem? Breathe And Know That You Are
Perfect In This Moment.

#351

Set Your Goals High And Do Something Every Day To Move Forward.

#352

In Every Moment, For Every Reason, Choose LOVE.

#353

May You Recognize The Passion And The Possibility In Your Day Today And Have The Courage To Follow It.

#354

If We Aim High And Fall Short, We Still Achieve More Than By Aiming Low And Falling Short.

#355

In All Moments, For All Reasons, Love Completely.

#356
Refuse To Be Defined By Someone Else's
Vision Of What's Possible.

#357
Your Words Are Simply The Thoughts Of
Yours That Will Become Things The Soonest.

#358
Having A Great Dream And Belief In Yourself
Is Great, But Nothing Happens Until You Take
Action.

#359
Life Is About Right Now In This Very Moment.
Not Tomorrow, Not Yesterday But NOW. Live
It!

#360
Follow Your Passion. Listen To Your Heart.
Trust The Process. Be Grateful. Life Is Magic
And Your Dreams Matter.

#361
Who And What You Are Will Be Determined By You, Not By Your Circumstances.

#362
The Greatest Personal Fulfillment Comes When We Contribute To Improving The Welfare Of Others.

#363
In Every Moment, You Are The Only One Who Gets To Choose Your Attitude. Choose Wisely.

#364
Trust Is Knowing That We're Exactly Where We Are Supposed To Be In Life, Especially When It Doesn't Feel Like It.

#365
Do what you can, with what you have, where you are.

Please Leave A Review!

I would be incredibly thankful if you take just 60 seconds to write a brief review on Amazon, even if it is just a few positive words.

Conclusion

I hope you have gained inspiration, motivation, success and happiness from the quotes you have read in this book. My aim with this book was to help anyone that just needed to have just a few positive words each day in their life to help them become the best version of themselves.

If you can please spare 60 seconds to leave a positive review on this book so I can help even more people with the positive words found inside.